The Lift

Julian Thomlinson

Series Editors:
Rob Waring and Sue Leather
Series Story Consultant: Julian Thomlinson

NATIONAL GEOGRAPHIC LEARNING | CENGAGE Learning·

Australia • Brazil • Japan • Korea • Mexico • Singapore • Spain • United Kingdom • United States

Page Turners Reading Library
The Lift
Julian Thomlinson

Publisher: Andrew Robinson

Executive Editor: Sean Bermingham

Editorial Assistant: Dylan Mitchell

Director of Global Marketing:
Ian Martin

Senior Content Project Manager:
Tan Jin Hock

Manufacturing Planner:
Mary Beth Hennebury

Contributor: Vessela Gasper

Layout Design and Illustrations:
Redbean Design Pte Ltd

Cover Illustration: Eric Foenander

Photo Credits:
42 Cedric Weber/Shutterstock
43 Andrey Bayda/Shutterstock
44 Diego Cervo/Shutterstock
45 Leah-Anne Thompson/Shutterstock

For permission to use material from this
text or product, submit all requests online
at **www.cengage.com/permissions**
Further permissions questions
can be emailed to
permissionrequest@cengage.com

ISBN-13: 978-1-4240-4887-8

ISBN-10: 1-4240-4887-7

National Geographic Learning
20 Channel Center Street
Boston, Massachusetts 02210
USA

Cengage Learning is a leading provider of
customized learning solutions with office
locations around the globe, including
Singapore, the United Kingdom, Australia,
Mexico, Brazil, and Japan. Locate your local
office at:
international.cengage.com/region

Cengage Learning products are represented in
Canada by Nelson Education, Ltd.

Visit National Geographic Learning online at
NGL.Cengage.com

Visit our corporate website at
www.cengage.com

Printed in the United States of America
2 3 4 5 6 7 20 19 18

Contents

Background Reading

People in the story

Cameron (Cammy) Bailey
a second-year student at
Brenton College

Hilary Johnson
Cameron's rich friend and
a fellow student

Chris Chang
Cameron's boyfriend, who is
studying computers at Brenton

Tom Johnson
Hilary's father, a very
successful businessman

The story is set in Brenton, a college town in the
northwestern United States.

Chapter 1

The sale

The problem with shopping, thinks Cameron, standing in Seattle's most expensive department store, *is it costs too much money.*

She didn't even want to leave the house this weekend. It was halfway through the semester, and to find money was getting difficult. She was just going to stay home and do some work.

That was before her best friend Hilary called around one o'clock and said, "Hey, Cammy, there's a sale on at Linden's."

So here she is at Linden's, on Saturday afternoon, a new top in her bag, wanting to get home before she buys anything else. Her friend Hilary isn't going anywhere. She's holding up two swimsuits—one blue, one red—and saying, for maybe the tenth time, "Cammy, I just can't decide."

"How much are they?" Cameron asks.

"The blue one is . . . $130. The red's $170."

"I thought they were on sale!"

"These are on sale," Hilary says.

$130 for a swimsuit?

"Why don't we go get a drink or something, and think about it?" Cameron says.

"I'll try them on again," Hilary replies, and goes back into the dressing room.

Cameron's legs feel as though she just ran a marathon, so she finds an empty chair and sits in it. She takes her shoes off and puts her legs out in front of her. That feels good. She looks up at the clock. It's 4 p.m. They've been in Linden's an hour and a half.

How does Hilary keep going like this? Cameron asks herself. Hilary's one of those people who always does everything 100%. She never wants to just sit and relax. She's always doing something—going running, making food, studying, or whatever. It makes Hilary a really interesting and fun friend, but Cameron sometimes wishes they could just sit down and talk. They never seem to do that. She puts her shoes back on and goes to see Hilary in the dressing room.

"How are you doing in there?" Cameron says through the door.

"Oh, I don't know," Hilary says. "Give me a few more minutes."

"I'm going to the café on the first floor," Cameron says. "I need something to drink before I fall over."

"Let's not go here. I don't like the café here," Hilary says. "Why don't you go to the Ruby? You know the one on Fourth Avenue? I'll meet you there in five minutes."

"OK."

Cameron heads to the café, staying away from the shoes, and walks down Seneca Street onto Fourth Avenue. There's one free table, by the window, so she puts her bag on it and gets a drink.

Five minutes go by, then ten, but Hilary doesn't come. Cameron finishes her drink and is going to call her, when Hilary, with a big smile on her face, taps on the window.

"Sorry for making you wait," Hilary says from the other side of the glass.

"Do you want to get something?" Cameron asks her.

"Do you mind if we just go? It's getting late."

"Sure," Cameron says, getting up. When she gets outside, she sees Hilary doesn't have any shopping bags, just the bag she came with.

"So you didn't get anything?" Cameron says.

"Look," Hilary says.

She opens her bag, and there's the red swimsuit.

"You think it's nice, don't you?" Hilary says.

"Yeah, it's nice," Cameron says, thinking it's strange

she doesn't have a Linden's bag. "Where's your bag?"

"Oh, I didn't want one," Hilary says, looking away suddenly. "Can we just go now, please?" Hilary starts walking away.

There's something wrong about this, Cameron thinks. *Why is Hilary being so strange?*

Hilary, Cameron thinks, *you didn't just steal that, did you?*

Chapter 2

Following

The idea of Hilary stealing something seems strange to Cameron. Hilary doesn't need to steal anything. Her father is the owner of a big west coast supermarket business. Her family has lots of money. Why is she going to steal a swimsuit when she can easily just buy it?

Thinking that Hilary maybe just stole something doesn't make her feel good, so she tries not to think about it. She says good-bye to Hilary, goes home and gets changed, then meets her boyfriend, Chris, for a drink. The next day she does some work, then goes to a movie with her friends Belinda and Katy. She has a few busy days at college, and as the week goes on, she forgets all about what she saw.

On Thursday evening she's on her way to get a bus to her sister's place when she sees Hilary across the street. At first she isn't sure it's Hilary at all. The girl she sees looks like Hilary, but there is something different about her. Hilary always seems so full of life, but the girl across the street isn't like that at all. She's walking very slowly, just looking down at her feet.

Wow, Cameron thinks, *she doesn't look very happy.* Cameron starts across the road, and is about to shout hello to her friend, but then she remembers the swimsuit and stops. She knows it's not good to follow your friends around, but something makes her just want to walk behind Hilary for a while and see what she's doing.

Hilary doesn't seem to be going anywhere. She looks in a few store windows, and one time she turns back to look behind her. Cameron stops, sure Hilary must see her. But she doesn't—Hilary looks right at Cameron, but it's as if she looks through her. She doesn't even see that she's there.

Cameron doesn't like seeing Hilary like this. She's about to run over and ask if she's OK, but before she can, Hilary turns into Linden's department store.

Cameron follows her up to the women's clothes on the second floor. Hilary looks at some shoes for a while, then goes to look at some scarves. She's picking up scarves and holding them up to look at them. She picks up a dark green scarf, and without even looking around, puts it into her bag. Cameron can't believe what she's seeing.

Without hurrying at all, Hilary turns and heads down the stairs. Cameron follows her out the front doors, and by the time she's on the street, Hilary's

walking much faster. It's as if taking the scarf has given her life.

Cameron runs up behind her and touches her on the back. Hilary turns around, her face white, but then seeing it's her friend, she breaks into a smile.

"Hey, Cammy," Hilary says happily. "What are you doing here?"

"What am I doing?" Cameron asks. "Hilary, what are *you* doing?"

"What am I doing about what?"

"In there," Cameron says. "In Linden's. I saw what you did."

"Are you following me?" Hilary says.

"No!" Cameron says. "I mean, not really. I saw you in the street and I went in the store to find you, and . . ."

"You *were* following me."

"I was coming to speak to you," Cameron says.

"I was in there ten minutes," Hilary says. "Why didn't you say something?" She isn't smiling anymore. She's looking at Cameron as if she doesn't know who she is. When Cameron looks at Hilary's face, the only word she can think of is *cold*.

"I wanted to," Cameron says. She can't think of what to say. She's starting to feel like she did something wrong. Before she can think of anything better, she says, "I just saw you steal a scarf, Hilary."

"Are you crazy?"

"Hilary," Cameron says, suddenly feeling very tired. "I saw you."

"I don't know what you think you saw, Cameron," Hilary says, "but you're wrong."

"You stole that swimsuit, didn't you? On Saturday?"

"I didn't steal anything!"

Cameron opens Hilary's handbag. The scarf's there, right on top.

"What's this, Hilary?" Cameron says. Hilary pulls her handbag shut, and looks left and right along the street. "I'm your friend. I'm on your side. What are you doing?"

"You're not my friend," Hilary shouts. "Don't say that you're my friend. You are not my friend."

"Hilary, don't say that," Cameron says. "Talk to me."

"I don't want to talk to you," Hilary shouts, walking away from her. "Get away from me."

"Wait," Cameron says. "Don't go, Hilary."

Hilary just keeps walking.

Chapter 3

Why

After she finishes class the next day, Cameron meets her boyfriend, Chris, at lunchtime. It's a hot, sunny day so they get sandwiches and sit under the trees near the fountain. Chris is saying something about his college paper, but Cameron's not really listening. She can't stop thinking about what happened.

"You know," Chris says, "sooner or later you're going to have to tell me what's wrong."

"What do you mean?" Cameron asks.

"I think I know you by now. I can tell when something's wrong."

"It has nothing to do with us," she says. "Really."

"OK," Chris says. "Well, I'm just saying I'm here, if you want to talk."

Cameron doesn't want to say anything about Hilary, but she does want to do the right thing. *Chris is smart,* she thinks. *He may know what to do.*

"Imagine one of your good friends does something bad," she says. "She—or he—does something wrong, something that can get her in trouble. Or him in trouble."

"What did she do?"

"I'm not saying it's a she," Cameron says. "I'm not saying anybody did anything. I'm saying . . . imagine."

"OK," says Chris. "I'm imagining. What did they do?"

"Imagine they steal something," Cameron says.

"What, like from another person?"

"A store," Cameron says. She can't help looking behind her as she says it. "Stealing clothes from a store. And not just one thing. Lots of things, I think."

"So they're shoplifting," Chris says, thinking about it. "You know, when people talk about their friend doing something wrong, it usually means *they're* doing something wrong. You're not saying you're stealing from stores, are you?"

"No! Really. It's not me."

"It's really not you?" Chris says.

"It's really not me," Cameron replies.

"OK," Chris says. "Well, of course, they have to stop doing it. You have to talk to them. Do you know why?"

"I have no idea why she's doing it," Cameron says.

"It's a she, then," Chris says. *Be careful, Cammy,* Cameron thinks to herself. *If you're not smart about it, Chris will know whom you're talking about.* "What kind of clothes?"

"The expensive kind."

"Is she stealing them to wear or to sell?"

What a strange question, Cameron thinks. "To wear, of course."

"It's not so simple, Cammy. If someone has got really bad money problems, they don't steal clothes to wear. They steal them to sell so they can pay for food and things."

"No, no," Cameron says. "This person does not have money problems. Anything she's stealing, she could buy if she wants to."

Chris thinks for some time before he says, "I think when people with money go out and steal things from stores, they're doing it because they have some kind of problem. Do you remember when that Hollywood star got caught for shoplifting?"

"Liz Long?" Cameron says.

"That's her," Chris says, taking out his phone. "Let me have a look."

Chris looks through some web pages on his phone, then shows her a news story. It reads: *"Unhappy Liz Long says that shoplifting gave her 'a lift.'"*

The story talks about how Liz Long was unhappy because things were bad with her husband, and that she started shoplifting because it excited her and made her feel better. Cameron remembers how unhappy Hilary looked before she went into Linden's.

"What's she unhappy about?" Cameron says, more to herself than to Chris. It's not an easy question to answer. Hilary is one of those girls who always seem as though they have it all. Cameron continues reading. There's a happy ending to the story. It seems that, after the arrest, Liz Long's life got much better. Cameron reads out loud the last part.

"*'It was just what I needed,' Liz said,*" Cameron reads. "*'In the end, getting caught was a good thing.'*"

"So maybe my friend needs to get caught? Maybe that's a good thing?" Cameron says.

"Maybe," says Chris. "Maybe not. Your friend's not a Hollywood star. She may have to leave college. She may go to jail. Do you see what I'm saying? If your friend gets caught, it may be really bad for her. It only takes one thing to make your life go wrong. One bad choice. Does she really want to take that chance?"

No, Cameron thinks. *She does not.*

Oh, Hilary.

What are you doing?

After Chris leaves, Cameron picks up her phone and finds Hilary's number. As she's waiting she wonders if Hilary will still be angry, but then Hilary answers and says, in a happy voice, "Hi, Cammy, how are you?"

"Hilary, is that you?" asks Cameron.

"Of course it's me. You're calling my phone, aren't you?"

"I just thought, after the other day . . ."

"I forgot about that already," Hilary says. "I meant to call you, to say sorry. I feel bad about what I said. I didn't mean it."

"I'm so happy you said that," says Cameron, though something about it didn't seem right. "I'm sorry as well. I mean, I wasn't following you or anything though."

"Don't worry," Hilary says. "I know it's kind of stupid. Are you free after class tomorrow? Let's do something."

"That'd be great," Cameron replies. "I'm going to my sister's house in Seattle but I'll be free about seven."

"Even better," Hilary says.

Chapter 4

The police

The phone call makes Cameron think that maybe Hilary's going to talk about things with her. She hopes that maybe now they can go for a coffee and Hilary will tell her a bit about herself, that she'll open up to her. But the first thing Hilary says is, "Do you want to go and see a movie?"

"Not really," Cameron says. "I thought maybe we could talk a bit. Go have a coffee somewhere?"

"Let's walk and talk," Hilary says.

"Don't you want to talk about, you know, last week?" Cameron says as they head down Seneca Street.

"Let's just forget it," Hilary says. "If that's OK with you. I'm sorry for getting angry with you. Really."

"Don't you think it may help to talk about it? I was thinking maybe you're unhappy about something. That if you want to talk to me about that, maybe I can help."

"I'm fine," Hilary says. "I'm perfect. Don't worry."

"OK," Cameron says. "But if there's anything you want to tell me . . ."

"Sure," Hilary says. But it seems like there isn't anything Hilary wants to tell her, or at least nothing important. She talks about her classes, about some new music she's listening to, about the movie she wanted to see. She even talks about her ex-boyfriend's new girlfriend, and Cameron thinks maybe that's the problem, but Hilary can't seem to stop laughing about it. By now they're outside Linden's.

"The sale's still on," Hilary says. "Let's have a quick look."

"You're not serious," Cameron says. Hilary laughs.

"I'm not going to do anything," she says.

"You really want to go in there?"

"Just for a quick look."

For the first time, Cameron sees the security man at the door as they go in. She wonders why she never saw him before. Going in Linden's gives her a strange feeling, but she follows anyway.

"I want to see some shoes," Hilary says, heading upstairs. Cameron's phone makes a sound. Chris is calling.

"I'll come in a minute," she says to Hilary.

Chris wants to know if they can study together tomorrow. As Hilary goes up the stairs, two of the store clerks look at her and start talking together fast. One of them picks up the phone.

"Can I call you back?" Cameron says to Chris. She finds Hilary looking at some beach shoes.

"I know what you're thinking," Hilary says. "Why am I looking at beach shoes?"

"Something's wrong," Cameron says.

"With beach shoes?"

"The store clerks downstairs. When they saw you they started talking."

"So? I'm not doing anything wrong."

"Maybe they remember you or something."

"They can't do anything if they don't see me do anything wrong," Hilary says. "I'm pretty sure about that."

"Can we just go somewhere else?"

Hilary looks a little angry, but she just says, "Sure."

The two of them go downstairs, but as they head for the doors, one of the women starts walking over to them, fast.

"Hilary?" Cameron says.

"It'll be fine," Hilary says. As they get to the door, the security man says, "Can I check your bags, please, ladies?"

"Why?" says Cameron.

"Sure," Hilary says, giving her bag to him. He looks through it slowly.

"There's nothing in there," says Cameron.

"I'm sorry, but would you please wait for a moment," says a voice from behind them. It's the store clerk.

"We need to go now," Hilary says. The security man is still looking through her bag. She says, "I'll have my bag back now, thank you very much."

"I'll have to ask you to stay for a moment," says the store clerk.

"Well, I'm not staying," says Hilary. "Get out of my way or I'll call the police."

"The police are on their way," the woman says.

"Why?" says Cameron, without thinking.

"This woman stole a scarf from our store last week. We have her on camera doing it. The police saw the video and were waiting for our call. They will be here in a moment."

"I did not," shouts Hilary. Some other people in the store are watching them.

"Hilary?" Cameron says.

"I didn't steal anything," Hilary says, "and you can't keep me here. Give me my bag and let us go."

"Miss, the police will be here soon. Why don't we go through to an office in the back and wait? You can see the video. It's very clear."

"I said, give me my bag!" Hilary says. She pulls the bag out of the man's hand and pushes past him out the door. The man doesn't try to stop her, but he follows her out.

"Hilary," says Cameron.

"Be quiet," shouts Hilary.

"The girl with the red bag," the big security man shouts, looking at Hilary. "There. Over there."

Everyone on the street stops and looks around. For a moment it seems like Hilary's the only one moving. There are two police officers across the street, looking toward them. *They can't be here yet,* Cameron thinks, but realizes there must be lots of police around the stores at this time. Hilary doesn't see them. One of the police officers, a woman, takes her arm gently and says something to her. The store clerk runs across the street and begins to talk to the police officers. They talk a little, but Cameron can't hear what they say. Hilary lowers her head as the officer brings her back toward the store, holding her arm.

Chapter 5

Dad

They aren't at the store for very long. As soon as the police officers see the video, they handcuff Hilary's hands and arrest her.

"Do you really need to do that?" Cameron says.

"Please move back," the officer says to her. They take Hilary out to the street. Cameron follows behind them.

"It's OK, Cammy," Hilary says. "Go home."

"Where are you taking her?" asks Cameron.

"The station on Fifth and Cherry," the officer replies.

They take her to a waiting police car. Cameron runs after them.

"Hilary!" Cameron says, as they put her in the car. "What do I do?"

Hilary doesn't reply.

Cameron hurries to the police station, thinking. Does she call Hilary's mother and father? She guesses the police will let Hilary call them, but maybe they'll make her wait a long time first. Cameron doesn't want to be the one to tell Hilary's mother or father that the police arrested their daughter for shoplifting, but they're going to find out anyway. She takes out her phone and calls Hilary's home number. After a few moments, a voice says, "This is Tom Johnson."

"Um, Mr. Johnson," Cameron says, "I'm Cameron Bailey, Hilary's friend from college."

"What can I do for you, Miss Bailey?" Mr. Johnson says. Hilary's father speaks very slowly, as if he wants you to listen very carefully.

"Mr. Johnson, I'm very sorry to be calling you, but I've just left Hilary in town and . . . I'm really sorry to tell you this, but Hilary was arrested. For stealing things from Linden's, the department store. Mr. Johnson, can you hear me?"

"I can hear you very well," Mr. Johnson says. "And the police took her where? The central station?"

"That's right," Cameron says.

"Thank you," Mr. Johnson says, putting down the phone.

Well, that was . . . strange, Cameron thinks. She's almost at the police station now and she thinks about what to do.

Maybe you need to go home, she thinks. *Just go home and stay out of it.*

Instead she goes inside.

It's not what she thought—it's more like a hotel than a police station. Hilary's not around, and Cameron guesses she's in one of the back rooms somewhere. She joins a line of people waiting to talk to a police officer sitting behind a window. After a while, Cameron gets to speak to him, but he just tells her to wait.

So she waits. Everybody in the room is sitting quietly, reading or looking around. She wonders why they are there. Now and again the police bring in someone, but nobody's shouting or getting angry. At one moment, a big, gray-haired man in a business suit comes in, and Cameron wonders if it's Hilary's father. She thinks about speaking to him, but before she can, they take him inside to one of the rooms in the back.

An hour goes by. Cameron tries Hilary's phone every 20 minutes or so, but there's no answer. Just when she's starting to think they're keeping her in all night, Hilary comes out of one of the rooms in the back with the businessman holding her arm, a cold look on his face. Cameron gets up.

"Hilary," she says.

"Hi," Hilary says. "When did you get here?"

"I was worried about you," Cameron says. "What's happening?"

Before Hilary can reply, the tall man says, "Get in the car, Hilary."

"The store wants to take me to court," Hilary says. "I have to go in a couple of weeks. The police say because I did it more than once, I could even go to jail."

Chapter 6

Friends

Mr. Johnson's car is big and European, and nobody says anything as they get into it. Cameron wants to ask what happened, but she doesn't want to be the first to speak, and she can tell Hilary's father is very angry. Hilary's eyes are dark from crying. Cameron wants to say something that'll make her feel better, but she doesn't know what that is.

It takes about half an hour to get to Cameron's place, but they're nearly there and still nobody's speaking. *Maybe I should just get a bus,* Cameron's thinking, but just as she's about to tell Mr. Johnson he doesn't need to drive her home, Hilary says, "I'm sorry, Daddy."

Mr. Johnson doesn't reply.

"Daddy, I said I'm sorry."

"Just tell me why," her father says. "Why did you do it?"

"I don't know," Hilary says.

"You don't know?" he replies. "You don't know? You've brought this on everyone in this family and when I ask you why, you say you 'don't know'?"

"Dad, please don't make this worse," Hilary says.

"Make it worse? Do you know what you've done? This is going to follow you around all your life. They have video of you stealing from the store, a number of times."

"What do you care?"

"What do *I* care? Of course I care. You're my daughter. And it's not just you. People will talk. Can you imagine what it's going to be like for me? What about Eric? What about when his school friends find out? Do you think the mothers and fathers will want their sons or daughters to be friends with a boy whose sister steals? And the newspapers? Oh, the newspapers will have a great time with this."

"Stop it, Dad," Hilary says. "Don't bring Eric into this."

"You know how people are. And what about your mother? What do you think she would say, if she were still with us?"

"Stop it," Hilary says, her voice breaking now. "It's nothing to do with Mom."

Yeah, stop it, Cameron's thinking. *Can't you see she's upset?*

"She would think badly of you, Hilary," Hilary's father says. Cameron thinks she's never heard such a cold voice. Hilary starts to cry, and Cameron thinks, *I think I understand, Hilary. I think I know why you're doing it. I'm just sorry I didn't know before.*

"Stop it!" Hilary shouts, crying now. "Don't say that."

Cameron puts a hand on her shoulder.

"Yeah, stop it," Cameron says. "You don't need to talk to her like that."

"Young lady," Mr. Johnson says, "this has nothing to do with you, so please be quiet. We'll continue this at home, Hilary. Cameron, I believe this is your apartment."

"Can I stay with you, Cammy?" Hilary says.

"Did you not hear what I just said?" her father says.

"Sure you can," Cameron replies. She gets out of the car.

Hilary looks at her and mouths the words "thank you." Mr. Johnson reaches over Hilary and pushes open the door on her side of the car.

"Go on, then. You, too. Get out," he says. "You're a big girl. You can do what you want."

"I'm sorry, Daddy," Hilary says, getting out of the car and closing the door behind her.

Mr. Johnson looks at Hilary. *His face is different,* Cameron thinks. Not cold anymore, just . . . sad. *He seems like a very unhappy man,* Cameron thinks. It's just for a moment, and it's as if he's about to say something, then changes his mind. The big car pulls away. The cold air feels good on Cameron's face.

They go inside and sit on Cameron's bed.

"He never used to be like that," Hilary says. "When I was young, he was always laughing. But when Mom died, he really changed."

"When was this?" Cameron asks her. "Is it OK for me to ask?"

"Of course it is. It was three years ago, in September. September 21, it was. She was sick for years, but . . . we were all really strong together and I thought we'd be OK, but everything changed. It was Dad, mostly. After that, he just worked all the time. We almost never saw him. We never talked about Mom. We never talked about anything. That was why I got so upset today. It was the first time he talked about her in ages."

"That's why you were doing it, isn't it? Because of your mom?"

"I used to think it was about Mom," Hilary says. "But now I think it's just as much about Dad. I miss him, too. He's so cold now. It's like he doesn't even see me some of the time. I just wanted him to talk to me. I guess he's talking to me now, huh?"

"Why didn't you say something?" Cameron says. "Maybe not to me, but someone. You know, talking to someone can really help."

"I didn't want anybody to know," Hilary says. "I thought if anybody knows what I'm really like, they won't want to be friends with me."

"It's not like that at all," Cameron says. Hilary looks so tired.

"Sleep," Cameron says.

"Is that OK?" Hilary says.

"Sure. You can have my bed. I'll sleep in the other room."

"Are you sure?"

"Yes, I'm sure," Cameron says.

Hilary puts her head down and closes her eyes, but only for a moment.

"Do you think it'll be OK?" she says, in a voice that sounds like a child's.

"The first thing tomorrow, go and talk to your dad. Tell him what you just told me. Do you think you can do that?"

Hilary thought about it for a while.

"I guess so," Hilary says.

"Then I think it'll be OK. It won't be easy, but you'll get through it. I know you will."

Hilary smiles then.

"You're such a good friend, Cammy," she says. "When I go to court, I really hope you can come with me."

"Don't think about that now," Cameron says.

Hilary closes her eyes. Cameron stays with her a moment, watching her friend, thinking how small she looks, lying there like that. She watches a moment more, then goes through to the other room, makes a bed on the sofa, and lies down on it. For a while she just lies there, looking up at the ceiling, her eyes open.

Review

A. Match the characters in the story to their descriptions. Use the names in the box.

Cameron	Hilary	Chris	Tom

1. _____ is Cameron's boyfriend.

2. _____ follows Hilary into the store.

3. _____ steals things from the department store.

4. _____ speaks to her boyfriend about a friend who is stealing.

5. _____ advises his girlfriend.

6. _____ may have to leave the university.

7. _____ is very successful in business.

8. _____ is worried about what the newspapers will say.

B. Read each statement and decide whether it is true (T) or false (F).

1. Cameron and Hilary are best friends.   T / F

2. Hilary steals a jacket and a scarf.   T / F

3. Cameron thinks her boyfriend is stealing things.   T / F

4. The store uses cameras to catch people stealing.   T / F

5. The police make an arrest inside the store.   T / F

6. Tom is very cold to Hilary.   T / F

7. Hilary spends the night at Cameron's apartment.   T / F

8. Hilary must go to court soon.   T / F

C. Choose the best answer for each question.

1. Linden's _____ .

    a. is a brand of swimsuit

    b. is the name of a department store

    c. is Tom's company's name

2. Chris _____ .

    a. helps Cameron talk about what she saw

    b. drives Cameron home from the police station

    c. is Hilary's brother

3. Cameron _____ .

    a. wants to help Hilary

    b. is shocked to find the swimsuit in her own bag

    c. is arrested by the police

4. Hilary _____ .

    a. is worried about Chris

    b. loses all her friends at the end of the story

    c. is in trouble with the police because of her actions

5. Tom _____ .

    a. is happily married

    b. tries to come home early every day so he can see his daughter

    c. works so hard that he has no time for his daughter

6. Tom _____ .

    a. is worried about his business

    b. is worried that Eric's school friends will find out about Hilary

    c. wants to write to the newspapers

D. Number these events in the order they happened (1–8).

a. Hilary looks sad walking in the street. _____

b. Cameron calls Hilary's father. _____

c. Cameron sees a new swimsuit in Hilary's bag. _____

d. Cameron and Hilary have a fight. _____

e. Cameron goes to the police station. _____

f. Hilary and Cameron talk about Hilary's mother. _____

g. The security man speaks to Cameron and Hilary. _____

h. Cameron watches her friend sleep. _____

Answer Key

A:
1. Chris; **2.** Cameron; **3.** Hilary; **4.** Cameron; **5.** Chris; **6.** Hilary; **7.** Tom; **8.** Tom

B:
1. T; **2.** F; **3.** F; **4.** T; **5.** F; **6.** T; **7.** T; **8.** T

C:
1. b; **2.** a; **3.** a; **4.** c; **5.** c; **6.** b

D:
a. 2; **b.** 5; **c.** 1; **d.** 3; **e.** 6; **f.** 7; **g.** 4; **h.** 8

Background Reading:

Spotlight on ... *Famous department stores*

The world has many famous department stores. Let's read about some.

Bennetts, Derby, UK

Bennetts is often said to be the world's first department store. It opened in 1734 and still does business in the same building. Many of the staff have worked there all their working lives.

Harrods, London, UK

Harrods first opened in 1834 and is internationally recognized. It is the world's high-class expensive department store where kings, queens, sultans, and emperors go shopping. It is also the biggest department store in Europe.

Galeries Lafayette, Paris, France

Galeries Lafayatte opened in 1895 as a small fashion store. It expanded rapidly with the purchase of several buildings outside Paris as well as outside of France. It is now a major department store. It is known for its amazing buildings and high-class atmosphere. You can buy brand-name products from all over the world.

Macy's, New York, USA

Until 2009, Macy's at Herald Square in New York was the world's largest store. Macy's now operates about 800 stores throughout the US and is known for its wide range of goods.

Shinsegae Centum City, Busan, South Korea

Shinsegae translates as "new world." This store opened in March 2009 with 294,000 square meters of shopping space and 509,800 square meters of floor space. It has many movie theaters, a skating rink, a spa, and a golf driving range in the store.

Amazon, Seattle, USA

Amazon is a new kind of department store that exists only online. There are no shops to walk around. Started in 1994, it originally sold books, but now it has become the world's largest online retailer, selling almost anything.

Think About It

1. Which of these stores would you most like to visit?
2. What kinds of problems do you think these stores will face in the future?

Spotlight on ... *Why do people steal?*

It's easy to think people steal because they are hungry, need things, or need money. But this is not always true. Many types of people steal; rich and poor people steal, old and young, good and bad people, too. Stealing is always bad, of course, but here are some reasons why people do it.

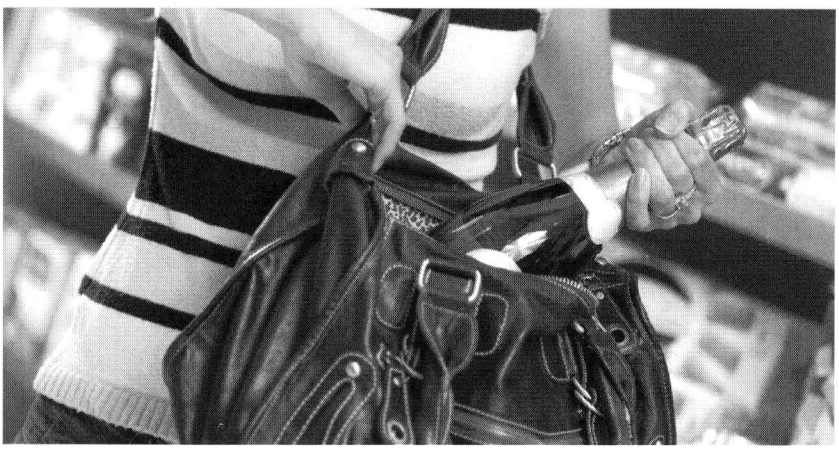

- They feel it is like getting a present, or getting something for free. If you win the lottery, you'd feel lucky and happy, but these people confuse stealing with luck.

- Some people are angry with someone and want to get back at them secretly by stealing from them.

- Some people steal to try to replace something they lost. They might steal because of someone who died, an illness, or the loss of a job.

- Some people may feel lost or lonely, and secretly want to get caught so they can get attention and be noticed.

- Sometimes, their friends have things they like, such as a phone, nice shoes, or nice clothes. They feel they should have them, too, so they steal these things to try to stay part of the group.

- Some people steal because they are bored or frustrated, and may feel excited by not getting caught. The problem is that these people feel the "high" from their actions and do it again and again.

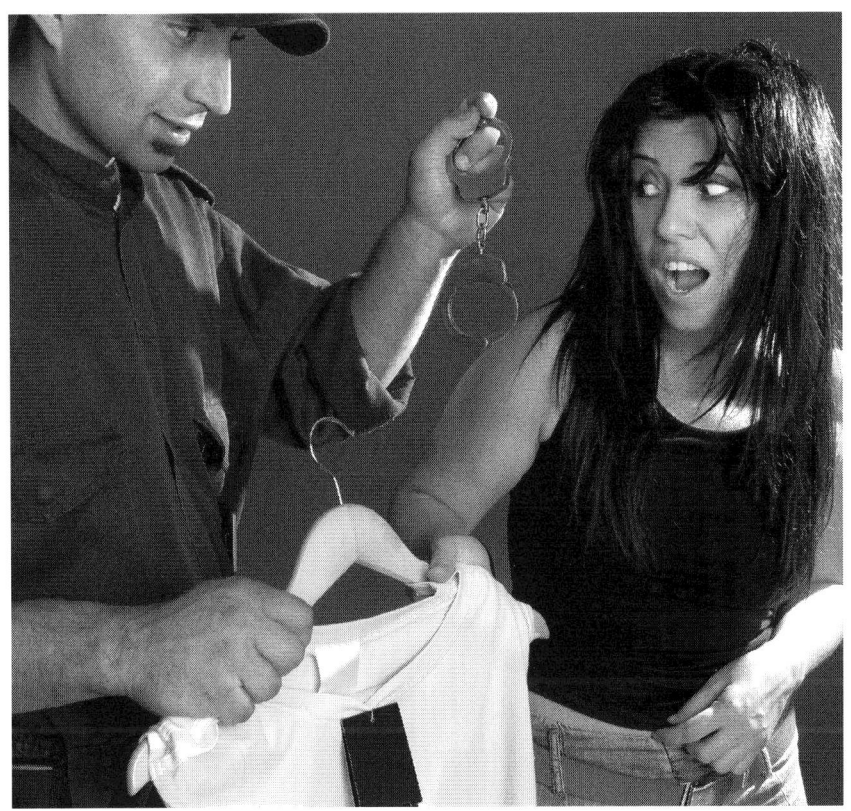

Often, people steal because they cannot handle their personal life situations. While it might be hard to change your life, stealing is not a way to make it better. It can make your life much worse.

Shoplifters need to find ways to deal with their life's problems directly by getting help from family, friends, or professionals.

Think About It

1. What would you do if you saw a shoplifter?

2. Think of some reasons why shoplifting is bad for society as a whole.

Glossary

arrest	(*v.*)	to take to or keep in a police station for breaking the law
department store	(*n.*)	a very large store that sells almost everything
handcuff	(*v.*)	to put handcuffs on someone
handcuffs	(*n.*)	a pair of metal rings that can be locked around someone's hands
hold	(*v.*)	to have something in your hand; to carry it
imagine	(*v.*)	to believe; to dream
jail	(*n.*)	a place to keep people found guilty of a crime
lift	(*n.*)	a rise in a person's mood that makes them feel better, happier
moment	(*n.*)	a short piece of time lasting a few seconds
perfect	(*adj.*)	pure, total, best
police officer	(*n.*)	someone who works for the police
sale	(*n.*)	a special time when stores lower their prices
scarf	(*n.*)	a piece of cloth worn around the neck or head
security	(*n.*)	in a department store, the people who make sure people are safe and are not stealing things
shoplifting	(*n.*)	stealing from stores
star	(*n.*)	someone famous like an actor or singer
steal	(*v.*)	to take something without paying for it
store clerk	(*n.*)	a person who works in a store
suit	(*n.*)	a jacket and pants or skirt for businesspeople
upset	(*adj.*)	sad or worried about something
wonder	(*v.*)	to think about something